# 19 High-Impact Study Hacks:

## Learn Techniques Top Students Use To Get Amazing Grades and Cut Study Time in Half

By Richard Glenn

Published by LearnU.org © 2014

# Introduction

I've been through the academic wringer. I've been a student at pretty much all education levels. I have two bachelor's degrees. I enrolled in one master's program before I dropped out (because I hated it and was bad at it) before regrouping and earning my MFA a few years later.

Eventually, I started teaching college classes. So I've been either a college student or a college instructor for about a decade. During that time, I developed tons of little tips and tricks—hacks, if you will—for studying.

When I became a teacher, I was pretty surprised to see how many of my students didn't know about these hacks. Most of them were just kind of slogging through school, doing every little assignment one by one, not at all worried about whether or not they were doing it efficiently.

So I sat down to write this book. Here, you'll find the first seven of my study hacks. These are some of the most effective techniques I developed to produce the greatest impact on my students' grades in the shortest amount of time.

All of these hacks take 30 minutes or less (except for a few of the paper-writing hacks). Most of them take less than 10 minutes and *save you more than 10 minutes*, which means you'll actually be spending *less* time studying.

But they all have one thing in common: they're designed to be quick, easy—even fun!—and drastically improve your grades. If you do them all, I'd wager you could raise your GPA by quite a bit over the course of a semester.

In any case, I hope you find them useful. They got me through a lot of tough semesters. If you have any hacks to add, please feel free to shoot me an email at admin@learnu.org.

Or you can just stop by our site at Learnu.org to chat with us there.

Thanks for reading, and enjoy!

Richard

# Table of contents

# Time Management Hacks

Next to the psychology section, this is one of the most important sections in this book. Time management is often at the heart of every ultra-effective student. And when I say "time management," I don't mean putting studying before anything else. I don't want you to do that! I want you to not have to spend hours and hours studying, so you can actually have a life! What follows are some tips to help you do that.

## Hack #1: Use the **snowball method** when you have tons of homework.

This is actually something I stole from the personal finance world back in the day, and it's actually totally unrelated to studying. However, it's a really powerful antidote to that feeling of utter helplessness when you have a mountain of homework, and you just don't know how you're going to finish it in time.

**IN A NUTSHELL: When you have tons of homework, organize it from smallest/fastest/easiest to hardest/longest. Do the small ones first and work your way up.**

**Why?** The snowball method is really a psychology hack. If you've got five different assignments due for five different classes, it's very easy to get paralyzed with fear because it just seems impossible that any of it will ever get done. You look at your pile of homework, and you just see hours and hours of toil ahead of you. Then you shut down. You put it off. And you end up scrambling and crying at the last minute, turning in C+ work.

The most important thing about the snowball method is that it *helps you start*. Doing the smaller stuff first gets you going, and when you have tons of stuff to do, starting is absolutely critical.

The second most important thing about the snowball method is *momentum*. We've all felt this way before: that feeling of just being on fire and unstoppable – that feeling of just crushing your homework and nothing can get in your way. *That's momentum.*

The snowball method helps you manufacture your own momentum. If you knock out a few small tasks first, by the time you get to the big stuff, you're already in the groove, already running full speed.

**How?** Figure out what's the scariest to you and put that stuff last. Are the really hard assignments scariest? Do you just hate long assignments? Whatever it is that makes you *not* want to do it, put that stuff last. Often times, those will be the same thing.

Then work backwards. Figure out what the next most annoying thing is, and put that second to last.

After you've got it all organized, the single most important thing is to start on whatever assignment ended up being the easiest. *Just start.* Even if it's slow. Just start, and don't take a break until it's finished. If you don't knock out the first thing, you won't be able to leverage all of that momentum later.

**Shortcut:** This may not seem like a short cut, but trust me: it is. If you plan to really sit down for a snowball session, bring in some assignments that aren't due yet. The idea here is that you'll be so in a groove that you'll just be knocking stuff out left and right. So why not do some more work while you're here? It will save you from having to get *back into the groove* later. If you do this on a regular basis, you can sometimes get away with just doing all of your stuff on one or two nights a week.

**Bonus!** If you find that you like the snowball method, try its sister method, the avalanche method. This is like the snowball method but opposite. Instead of starting with the easiest thing first, you start with the most difficult.

The idea here is that after you complete the most difficult thing you have to do, all the rest of the stuff seems easy. Both work, and usually it's just a matter of figure out which is best for your specific study personality. I personally like the avalanche method, but most people usually like the snowball method. So give them a try!

## Hack #2: Supercharge time management by **associating studying with other activities**.

Have you ever read that old adage that says that for something to become a habit, you have to do it for a full month? Studying can be the exact same. Before you slam your Kindle down in disgust, let me be clear: I'm not saying you have to study every day!

For Pete's sake, who would ever want to do that? I sure don't, and I'd never recommend it. However, you can still make studying a part of your routine without having to totally overwork yourself. And you can do it by associating it with other activities.

**IN A NUTSHELL: Pick an activity you do all the time (nearly every day) and study during that time to create both a positive association and a habit.**

**Why?** Creating an actual study *habit* is one of the most incredibly difficult things to do. Some people don't have a hard time with it. My college roommate, for example, would get up at 7:00 every single morning—even Saturdays!—to do his homework for the next day.

It's hard because you have to do something consistently to make it a habit, and everyone hates studying. It's often just easier to suffer through hours of studying before the test than it is to inject studying into your daily routine.

This tip is about doing just that—injecting studying into your routine—in a fun, low-stress way. You do it through *association*.

Associations are a psychological phenomenon that "refers to a connection between conceptual entities or mental states that results from the similarity between those states." In other words, you want to associate studying with something else.

If you do that, every time you do that thing, whatever it is, you'll think about studying. Not only will this help you remember to study, but it will also create a *positive* association with studying.

**How?** Pick something you do daily (or almost daily). Ideally, it should be something you really like doing as well as something you can do while studying. For me, it was Netflix. I always spend a few minutes every day watching shows on Netflix.

Then, make a point for one month to bring your study materials with you when you do that thing. You don't have to study super hard or anything; just study while you do that thing. Eventually, it'll become a low-stress but highly consistent habit!

**Pro tip!** If you really want to create a strong association, pair your studying with food. Even better, pair it with food *and* something else. So, for example, if you eat a little chocolate every day, and you watch Netflix every day, add studying to the mix.

This works particularly well because your brain forms much strong associations with tastes and smells than it does with other things.

# Psychology Hacks

This is probably one of the most important chapters in this book. To really become a great studier, you need to be able to wrangle your own brain. And to do that, you have to understand how it works. There are countless psychological study tactics you can use. These are just some of the ones I've found most useful over the years.

## Hack #3: Use **mnemonic devices** (and make them dirty).

There are tons and tons of books you can read about memory and mnemonic devices. We're not going to regurgitate all that information here. Instead, we're going to give you a few condensed techniques that really worked for us.

**IN A NUTSHELL: The best mnemonic devices are the ones that are super outlandish. One of the best ways to make them outlandish is to just make them really naughty.**

**Why?** Over the course of a school year, you're going to have tons and tons of facts thrown at you. The sheer volume of information can be a major obstacle. In the short term, it can prevent you from, say, remembering things you might need to know for a test.

In the long term, though, it usually means that you don't remember the things you learn. I'm sure you know that feeling: you study all night for a test, and as soon as you finish it, your brain immediately scraps everything you've learned in a giant cognitive sigh of relief.

Mnemonic devices are a great biohack that breaks the cycle of forgetting what you just learned. And you really shouldn't underestimate the power of these guys; I still remember stuff I studied as I was preparing to take the GRE almost 10 years ago—all because I was using mnemonic devices.

**How?** At its heart, a mnemonic device is just an association. That means you take whatever you're trying to remember and tie it to something else in your brain. For example, if I wanted to remember what the word "divest" means (it means "to strip of"), I might imagine a big beefy guy in a vest stripping down in a funny way.

The idea is that whenever you see the word "divest," you immediate think of a big beefy guy in a vest stripping in a funny way, which in turn makes it easier to remember that the definition is "to strip of."

Did you notice how ridiculous the image was in this example? That's the hack here. Mnemonic devices work much, much better if the images you use are totally ridiculous. One of the best ways to do that, of course, is to make them super naughty.

This is a family-friendly book, so I'm not going to go into some of the images I use myself, but hopefully you can see what I'm talking about.

If you're not comfortable doing that (which is totally cool!), you can just shoot for something super, super outlandish. Here are a few ways to do that and how I'd use them to remember the definition of "divest":

- Create an image in a wild setting (a pilot in **vest** landing a plane on a **strip** made completely of jello... because it's on a planet made of jello)
- Go crazy with numbers (dressing in a nice **vest** and sitting down to a massive dinner plate with 1,000 **strips** of bacon)
- Make the size absurd (having a **vested** interest in a **strip** of bacon 5 miles long)

Hope you get the idea here, because these can be crazy powerful. And remember, this is only a brief example of how to use mnemonic devices. You should definitely learn more.

## Hack #4: **Study hard**, not long, using study "bursts."

A lot of students I talk to think studying hard means putting in a lot of hours, and that is absolutely not the case. In fact, if you study for a super long time, it may actually be *less* effective than studying really effectively for short bursts.

**IN A NUTSHELL: Study in short, ultra-efficient bursts rather than long sessions to remember more of what you learn.**

**Why?** Have you ever driven while tired? If you have, I hope you immediately pulled over. Studies have shown that driving tired is even more dangerous than driving drunk. Your attention span is drastically shorter, and you lose nearly all of your ability to focus.

Studying tired won't put anyone's life in danger, but it's effectively the same thing. If you're tired and bored, you can bet that your studying isn't going to be nearly as effective.

So, when you study, aim for short, powerful bursts. Do whatever works for you, but you can make these super short if you like. A study session as short as 5 minutes can be incredibly productive if it's well-organized and efficient.

This has an added bonus of making studying a lot less stressful. It's totally possible to study for 20 minutes out of an hour (within reason—not, like, if you're totally swamped) and send the rest of that hour watching Netflix and eating cookies.

Just be warned: *this will not work if you don't study really, really hard during those short bursts.*

**How?** The key to getting the most out of your short study bursts is being ultra-organized beforehand.

Before you get started, make sure you've got everything set up and organized according to what's most important to study. You want to put that stuff at the front and make sure all the materials are there.

When you launch into your hardcore study burst, you'll also want to have extremely specific things to do, so that you waste exactly zero time aimlessly looking over notes. That's not studying.

Instead, have one activity per thing. For example, if the most important thing for you to remember is the names of the first 10 American presidents, you might spend the whole 10 minutes of your first study burst outlining detailed mnemonic devices for each president.

Then, in the second burst, you might spend the whole 10 minutes saying those mnemonic devices out loud. Finally, in your third burst, you might spend the whole 10 minutes orating those things from memory.

Starting to make sense? The activities can be any strong studying tactic you like. The idea is to simply *take action during those bursts.*

**Pro tip!** If you have problems with stress, and you get anxiety before test, spread your study bursts over a longer period, giving yourself more rest in between. In those rest periods, do fun, distracting or relaxing things. The balance will help you when you *do* go back to studying.

## Hack #5: **Beat procrastination by NOT planning** (kind of).

Procrastinators *love* to plan. If you're a procrastinator, you know exactly what I'm talking about: you spend a whole day planning out exactly what you want to do to get everything done on time, and it looks totally perfect... and then you do nothing.

And believe me, it's not uncommon! There are plenty of procrastinators out there, including me! I had to learn the hard way over the course of several years (and particularly in my very first semester of college) that getting past procrastination was critical to getting good grades. So, here's what I found.

**IN A NUTSHELL: Stop planning and start doing. The worse you are at procrastinating, the less you should plan. Only plan after you've already started, and make your plans incredibly short.**

**Why?** Most of the time, procrastinators like to plan because it feels like we are getting stuff done, and we don't *actually* have to do any work.

This isn't a new phenomenon at all, either. Let me give you an example. You know how some people will decide to go on a diet, plan out their whole diet and exercise routine, and then tell everyone they know about how they're getting ready to do this epic, life-changing thing... and then just not do it?

Studies have found there's a very specific reason for this: when you tell people about what you're *going* to do, everyone will congratulate you on your motivation and tell you you're going to do a great job. Because of that, you get all the psychological benefits of having done it without actually having to do it.

Of course, if you are already psychologically satisfied with yourself, it becomes much more difficult to stay motivated. Why would you go bust your butt to do something when everyone's already told you good job?!

Procrastination with studying is very much the same—even if it's a bit more private. By planning your studying to death, you're essentially congratulating your brain on all the work it's done without having to really do anything!

**How?** So what should you do instead of planning? The short answer is to just not plan. Here's what I mean.

If you're a chronic procrastinator, the first and most important step is to stop planning and start doing. Realize that it's much more important to actually study than to plan, even if you feel like the studying is going to lack direction.

So just start at all costs. It usually helps to put less pressure on yourself. Just crack your book open for 5 minutes while you're watching a movie four days before the test. Then do it again at the end of the movie. You get the idea. Starting is the most important thing, and planning will make it hard to ever start.

Of course, planning can be very helpful. And you *should* do it... just not at the cost of studying. So, procrastinators should only plan after they've already started studying, and they should keep it very, very short. And I mean really short. Make a 5-point bullet list of the things you want to get done in that study session and no more! Planning for procrastinators is a death-trap, and it shouldn't take more than 30 seconds.

## Hack #6: **Gamify your studying** to make yourself ultra-productive.

Gamification is a relatively new phenomenon, but you can see it virtually everywhere. If you've ever played a game on social media, you've probably seen a bunch of the tactics before (e.g. "Share with three friends to unlock the super-pig game token!").

But it's not just for games anymore. It's spreading everywhere—and for good reason. Researchers have shown that it's an incredibly powerful motivational tool for pretty much any system in which things need to get done, including studying!

**IN A NUTSHELL: Set up small rewards for incremental tasks, giving yourself goals and rewards for getting stuff done.**

**Why?** Gamification is awesome for a few different reasons. First, it just makes everything more fun. And, if you couldn't already tell, making studying less of a drag is a major part of this book. Studying isn't inherently fun, but if we can make it at least a little amusing, we can usually get a lot more out of it.

Gamification does this, and it does it really well. Even gamifying your studying on a very small scale can have a pretty drastic impact on how it feels to actually do it; for me, gamification helped me truly enjoy some parts of my studying, which in turn helped me get much better grades.

Secondly, gamification, more than perhaps anything else, provides a *sense of accomplishment.* I really can't stress how important that is—especially for something like studying. In addition to just not being very much fun most of the time, studying can also feel futile.

And when something feels futile, it can be incredibly hard to stay motivated. If you add gamification into your study time, you can give yourself a sense of accomplishment, which can make it psychologically much easier to power through material, especially in longer sessions.

**How?** At its heart, almost all gamification systems are just series of rewards. Do this and get that. Do X, get Y. It's not very complicated at all.

And that's great news! It means that it's super easy for almost anyone to implement on a small scale. The important thing about this, though, is to give yourself awesome rewards. Having great rewards will make it super motivating.

Here's an easy example. One of my friends was a biochemistry major, and she had these massive textbooks with super dense material. So, one of her main homework tasks every night was just reading stuff that was very hard to read.

Her solution was to gamify it with... gummy bears! She put a gummy bear on top of each paragraph. She would then read the paragraph and repeat it aloud as if she was teaching the content to another person. After she did that, she got to eat the gummy bear for that paragraph. Pretty easy and pretty fun!

**Pro tip!** Mix up the rewards to supercharge the gamification effect. Give yourself small rewards for big tasks and a huge reward for completing a whole assignment.

If you're giving yourself gummy bears for reading paragraphs, take yourself and a friend to the movies for finishing three chapters. It can be anything as long as it feels like a big reward for you!

## Hack #7: **Repeat things out loud** to remember them more clearly.

Everyone knows there are different types of learnings: visual, auditory and kinesthetic. However, there's another type of learning that's not talked about too often that almost everyone benefits from: re-teaching.

That's the idea that if you learn something, you'll understand it much better if you re-teach it to someone else. For me, it's proven to be one of the best study tactics in my sturdy study toolbox.

**IN A NUSTSHELL: Repeat things out loud as if you were teaching them to someone else to gain a deeper understanding and commit them to memory.**

**Why?** Teaching things you know to someone else has a really cool effect on your brain. Usually, it's significantly more effective than just looking at stuff and trying to memorize it.

This is mostly because instead of just memorizing a fact, you are *explaining* it to someone. That means that you have to (1) put it into a context, (2) answer questions about it and (3) address gaps in your own knowledge that you may not have known existed.

It also gives your memory more things to hold onto when it's trying to recall information. For example, if you're taking a test, and you've got some flash cards rattling around in your brain, *and* you can remember the time you were explaining the French Revolution to your roommate, you'll have many more reference points.

I really wish I'd learned this sooner. I really only learned how effective this was when I became a teacher myself. And, man, after that first semester of teaching, I felt about a million times smarter (in my small little field, anyway).

**How?** There are a couple of different ways to do this, but the most important thing is that you're saying things out loud.

So, it's going to be slightly more effective if you actually have someone to teach your stuff to, but it's not necessary. Have a girlfriend or boyfriend? Make them sit down and listen to you talk about the French Revolution for a few minutes.

Have a roommate? Fix them dinner and force *them* to listen. You get the idea. Most of the time, people will be happy to help you out, especially if it only takes a few minutes, all they need to do is listen, and they get a free dinner!

However, you do this by yourself, too. Just stand up and explain it as if you were giving a speech or talking to a friend. An even better tactic is to try to explain it as if you were talking to a 6-year-old. This will force you to reduce the content to a very understandable level, which is a great mental exercise and requires a great deal of understanding.

# Reading Hacks

Reading is by far one of the most tedious tasks in basically any kind of school. The good news, however, is that most people go about reading in a very inefficient way. Here's a secret: reading every single word of every single book is *not* the best way to tackle reading! This chapter is all about tactics you can use to drastically cut down on the time you spend reading.

## Hack #8: Read the material **before** the lecture, not after.

This is one of the easiest, simplest things you can do to drastically improve your effectiveness as a student. In fact, it's *so* simple, I'm often baffled how many students don't do it.

**IN A NUTSHELL: Don't go to any lecture without reading the material you're going to be assigned beforehand. That way, the lecture isn't an introduction to the material; it's your first revision.**

**Time requirement:** 20-30 minutes, but it depends on the assignment.

**Why?** This is a comprehension thing, mostly. If you go into a lecture totally unprepared, having never heard anything about the material before, it's going to be much more difficult to understand. Even worse, you may be fumbling through notes, trying to find passages in a book, which means *you're not listening to the lecture.*

If you read the material you're *going to be assigned,* you'll already have a basic understanding of it before you even set foot in the classroom. So, instead of trying to juggle a bunch of stuff at once, you can really pay attention. Even more importantly, you'll probably have some really great questions that weren't answered when you were reading.

And it only makes sense, right? Who do you think would have a better understanding: the student who has read the material and actively engages in dialog with the professor about what he's read, or the student who's only half-listening and trying to catch up in the book. No brainer!

**How?** This is going to be easiest with classes that give you a syllabus, since most syllabi outline the reading and homework for each class period. Your goal isn't to read everything. You don't want to be super far ahead. You just want be one reading assignment ahead.

Suppose you're going to class on Tuesday, and you know by looking at the syllabus that you're going to have to read Chapter 8 for next Thursday. Read that chapter before the Tuesday class.

Additionally, I found it's best to do this the night before a class. Reading with no pressure (you don't have to read it; you're just getting ahead) can actually be pretty relaxing. Plus, reading the material and then sleeping on it will help you retain it.

**Shortcut:** Even if you don't want to (or don't have the time to) read the chapter beforehand, you should definitely skim it. We've listed some really great skimming techniques throughout this book, so that's a good place to start. Just, as always, be wary with skimming; if you're not careful, you may end up asking an obvious question. If you're going to skim, do it really well.

**Bonus!** As a bonus, find some other material on the subject that *isn't* reading. This is one of our favorite techniques, too, and with good reason. Giving yourself some kind of extra medium to process the information can drastically increase your understanding. So, after you read or skim that chapter, find yourself a YouTube video or a forum discussion to read. All of this usually takes 20-30 minutes, and you'll be shocked at how far ahead of your classmates you are.

# Hack #9: Learn the art of **skimming**.

You don't have to read everything. Yes, you heard that right. You don't have to read everything, and you're not slacking if you don't read everything. The idea that you have to read every word of every book you're assigned is a total myth, and, in my opinion, totally at odds with how the real world works.

But how do you not read everything and still contribute to discussions, write good papers, and complete assignments? Well, grasshopper, you do that by learning the dark art of **skimming.**

**IN A NUTSHELL: Instead of reading every word of the assignment, read the first and last sentences of each paragraph. As you go, pick out one or two important sections and read those in detail, making good notes.**

**Why?** This is a time management thing. Sometimes, the best way to study is to do things besides reading. Sometimes, the best way to study is to write, or think, or solve a problem. You can't do that if you've got your nose in a book.

Now, before I go on, I want to clarify because I really, really don't want you to misunderstand this. *Reading the material is important, and you're going to have to do it.* For some assignments, you won't be able to just skim, especially with, say, a computer science class.

However, for a lot of classes, you can be just as productive skimming as you would reading every word. In fact, in many cases, you can be *more* productive.

In the end, though, skimming allows you to drastically cut down on the time you spend reading without sacrificing the learning, which can free up more time for whatever mode of studying you find productive (or, heaven forbid, hanging out with your friends and enjoying yourself).

**How?** The idea here is not to read *nothing*. Rather, it's to reduce the amount of stuff you need to read by about half and still pick up about 95% of the stuff you need to know. Here's how you do it.

Read the introduction and the conclusion of whatever it is you're supposed to read, and *read them first*. Reading both the introduction and the conclusion first will give you a pretty good idea of what the piece is about overall, so as you skim, you'll be able to pick out what's important.

Then, read the first and last sentence of each paragraph. If you find a section that is particularly important, particularly difficult, or particularly interesting, read that section carefully, make a few notes, and write down a few follow up questions.

After you finish reading, take 2-3 minutes to write down your thoughts on what you just read and how it pertains to everything else you've learned in that class so far. This will help you *retain* all the stuff you just learned.

**Shortcut:** You can sometimes get away with reading just the first sentence of every paragraph. However, you probably won't understand the material as well. For some classes that's okay (e.g. a class in which the reading is supplemental). For some, though, that can really hurt you. So just be careful about it.

# Research Hacks

Researching is another time sink for a lot of people. Like with reading, though, it often takes a lot of time because (1) it's not fun, and (2) most people do it very inefficiently. This chapter is about improving your research skills, so you can research about twice as fast as your classmates and have a lot more fun doing it!

# Hack #10: Supplement your studying with **fun stuff**.

Hands down, one of the best things about being a student today is that you have access to the single most powerful learning tool ever created by man: the internet! And that means that it usually doesn't matter what you're learning about: you can usually find *something* about it on the internet, and a lot of the time, it's going to be a lot more fun than pouring over academic texts.

**IN A NUTHSELL: Find some other supplemental material (e.g. a YouTube video, forum discussion) that is fun for you, and use it to gain a better understanding of whatever you're learning about.**

**Why?** Listen, we've been real with each other, right? So let's be straight. Sometimes, some of the stuff you learn in a class is just... boring. However, sometimes, it's not the material itself that's boring; it might be the textbook, or the professor, or the article you're reading.

Almost all of the time, whatever you're learning about is out there on the internet, and there are cool, smart, funny people talking about it. Or making documentaries about it. Or singing about it.

Often, you can learn a lot more and have a lot more fun if you use these materials to gain a better understanding of the subject.

For example, I took a super, super boring French history class my freshman year of college. Everything about it was boring, right down to the outdated textbook we were using. However, there are tons and tons of documentaries on the internet about French history. When I started watching these, I found I actually really *liked* it. Not only was I learning a lot more than I would have if I'd just forced myself to read a bunch of boring books, but I found that those same boring books were a lot more interesting after watching a few really great documentaries.

**How?** You probably know where to find stuff on the internet by now, but I'll share a few of my favorite things anyway. The trick here is the find the thing that is most *fun* for you. Personally, I love movies. I also love talking to other people. So, when I was looking for some fun, supplemental material, I'd watch YouTube documentaries and find some interesting Reddit threads.

However, there are tons of great resources out there. Here are just a few.

- YouTube documentaries
- Reddit discussions
- Free online classrooms like Khan Academy or Academic Earth
- Emailing/skyping an expert (you'd be surprised how many are happy to chat with you)
- Wikipedia (no, it's not evil; more on this in a second)
- Blogs

**Shortcut:** There's no shortcut! That's kind of the beauty of this tip: it's totally optional. But making learning more fun is key to gaining a truly deep understanding of any subject. With the internet, you can totally do that for yourself. Pretty awesome, right?

## Hack #11: Use **Wikipedia.**

One of the things that annoyed me most in college was the attitude toward Wikipedia. You'll hear it in just about every class you're in: "Do not use Wikipedia as a source." Well, I wholeheartedly disagree; and, in fact, I think Wikipedia is one of the single greatest study tools ever made.

**IN A NUTSHELL: Use Wikipedia to (1) get a first, broad understanding of your subject and (2) find other amazing sources you can learn from.**

**Why?** Before we answer the question "Why use Wikipedia?" I think we first have the answer the question "Why is Wikipedia not evil?"

I'd imagine that any of the professors who condemn Wikipedia would be fine with you using an encyclopedia, right? In my view, any printed encyclopedia is not nearly as good of a resource as a constantly updated, constantly edited online encyclopedia that can gather information in real time.

The drawback, of course, is that anyone can edit it, which is why people are afraid of it. However, over the years, Wikipedia has proven remarkably efficient at retaining its intellectual integrity. In fact, its editors are almost infamous for ruthlessly cutting incorrect or unimportant content.

In short, Wikipedia will almost always be more comprehensive and up-to-date than most encyclopedias, making it at least a legitimate source, if not one of the best possible sources.

So use it! Even if your professors tell you not to, use it. You don't have to cite it. You don't have to use it as a source. But use it to supplement your learning, find sources in half the time, and participate in a good discussion. All of that will greatly help you study any subject.

**How?** Using Wikipedia is pretty simple. First, find the most related page to whatever it is you're studying, and read it. This won't take more than 10 minutes, and it'll give you a very, very good general understanding.

Then, use that page to find other related Wikipedia pages, and, if it makes sense, read those, too. For example, if you're learning about dogs, you might follow some internal links to pages on specific breeds or the history of dog domestication... whatever; you get the idea.

Finally, scroll down to the all-important sources section and see what you can find. Pick out and bookmark sources that meet the criteria for a citable source, so you can use them in future papers (or, if you're writing a paper, use this section to find your first source—or maybe even all of them).

**Shortcut:** I doubt you'll ever be so pressed for time that you can't read a Wikipedia page, but if you are, you can skim these just like you can anything else (remember our section on the art of skimming?). In fact, Wikipedia pages are usually *easier* to skim because they're so well structured.

**Bonus!** Wikipedia's not the only online encyclopedia. Did you know that the Encyclopedia Britannica is also online? It is. You can also try Reference.com and Encyclopedia.com, if you're in the mood for some more surfing.

# Class Hacks

Sometimes, your grades aren't 100% about what you do at home in front of your computer with a stack of books on your desk, it's about how you interact with people. These are some of my favorite hacks because they usually take very, very little time, and they can usually raise your grade in a class by a full letter grade. Check it out!

## Hack #12: Go **talk to your professors**!

This is one of those incredibly easy things that almost no one does. Believe me, I know. I taught college classes for a long time, and if I wanted my students to come talk to me, most of the time, I had to *force* my students to come chat with me.

This is mostly because no one likes going to their professor's office to talk. It can be weird, and it can be awkward. However, if you do it, you'll get a better grade nine times out of 10.

**IN A NUTSHELL: Go talk to your professors, even if it's just for 5 minutes per week. It can raise your grade even if you don't score any better on tests and papers.**

**Why?** I'm going to let you in on a little secret here, okay? This is a secret most professors don't want you to know about but they all talk about amongst themselves. In fact, it's something they worry about all the time. Ready?

A major part of grading is totally subjective.

This is much truer in the humanities than it is in the hard sciences, but it's true there too. And it's *even truer* if a class has a participation component, as most classes do nowadays.

What's that mean? Basically, because grading is always going to be subjective to some extent, professors will almost always give better grades to students who appear to be trying hard. And they'll give even better grades to students who appear to be trying *harder* than their classmates.

I know because I've done it. I've had B students who have gotten As because they were obviously trying really hard (and they'd usually improved a lot as a result).

And what's one of the best, easiest ways to show your professor you're trying and you care about getting a good grade? Go talk to them!

Popping by a professor's office once a week takes virtually no time at all, and it's a major signal to them that says, "Hey! I'm trying! I care!" Most of the time, that counts for a lot (because a lot of students just don't care).  Believe me when I say this can have a major impact—like, even a whole letter grade.

**How?** Take 5 minutes a week and stop by your professor's office during office hours. It doesn't have to be long. Just think of a few questions from the last lecture. Or ask about a recent paper. Anything works.

Just make sure not to overdo it. Professors are people, too, and if you're coming by their office every single day, it's probably too much. Once a week is more than enough.

**Pro tip!** If you want *even more* bonus points, go find a book or an article that your professor's published. Read it, and stop by their office to ask them questions about it.

You're not going to believe the response you get. Again, don't overdo it. Just ask a few questions you're generally curious about and try to relate them to the class. Trust me: it takes 5 minutes, and it will totally blow them away.

## Hack #13: **Take notes after the lecture**, not during the lecture.

This study hack is one of my favorites by far because it actually calls for you to do *less* work. Sign me up!

If you've ever been in a college classroom, especially in difficult classes, this scene probably sounds very familiar: the professor is standing in front of the class talking about whatever the lesson is that day, and all the students have their heads buried in their notebooks, frantically trying to scribble down every word he or she says.

When I was teaching college classes, I *hated* this. I always made my students stop doing that. Why? Because they were spending much more time trying to write stuff down than actually listening. What follows is a much better strategy.

**IN A NUTSHELL: Don't take any notes during a lecture if you can help it; instead, focus on listening and asking questions, and write notes immediately after the lecture.**

**Why?** For many of us (including me), it's tough to do several different things at once. And that's *especially* true if the two things you are trying to do are intellectual activities. Can you imagine trying to juggle and recite the Pledge of Allegiance?

This is kind of what it feels like when you're trying to take extensive notes while listening to a lecture. But there are lots of other drawbacks, too.

First, if you're focused on writing down what the professor says, you're almost always going to be behind what he or she's actually saying. So you're going to miss a lot. This is basically the opposite of what you want.

Plus, it's incredibly stressful, and eventually, you'll probably end up worrying about writing more than actually learning. Needless to say, that's far from the best way to learn!

**How?** Like I said, this is one of my favorite study hacks because it's remarkably simple. Instead of furiously taking notes in a lecture, focus on listening—*really listening hard*—to the lecture. Concentrate on it. Think about it. And, most importantly, *ask questions*.

What worked for me was to treat lectures like I was just having coffee with my professor and having an interesting conversation about an interesting topic. I treated it like I was just learning about something cool from someone who knew a lot about it.

With that mindset, not only is it easier to comprehend what you're hearing, but it's also less work and more fun.

You do need to take notes at some point, however. So, with this strategy, you just do it directly after the lecture. Timing is important here, since you want to get it down while it's still fresh in your mind.

This is how I'd do it. After the lecture, I'd take 5 minutes to write down the main points. Then, under the main points, I'd write down (1) the most interesting/important information for each one and (2) any questions I had/still have.

You'll find that your notes will be better, more concise, and much easier to read. Plus, when you go over them, you'll remember the lecture about a million times better!

# Hack #14: **Ask the best questions** in the class.

This is kind of like going to talk to your professors, and it has the same effect, but it takes even less time. This is all about that thing every professor wants these days: *participation*.

However, it's very important to realize that not all participation is created equal. There is definitely good and bad types of participation, and if you're a bad participator, you risk earning *negative* brownie points, which is pretty much the opposite of what you want.

But if you do it right, participating in class is an amazing way to boost your grade for virtually no effort.

**IN A NUTSHELL: Be the person in the class who asks the best questions and contributes the best comments. You don't have to talk a lot; you just have to say great stuff.**

**Why?** The reason this works is the exact same reason going to talk to your professors works: it shows that you are trying. More importantly, though, it shows that you're engaged in the class as it's actually happening.

And that's the big one. I can tell you from experience that one of the major struggles for most professors is making boring material interesting to a room full of college freshman. Who gets up in the morning and says to themselves, "I'm so pumped to learn about French history!" Maybe a few people, but certainly not most college freshmen.

If you can show your professor you are actively engaged in what they are saying, it will make you look like you're trying, sure, but it will also make them super grateful.

Isn't that crazy? By just asking a few questions or adding a comment, *you can make your professors feel thankful to even have you around.* That is a very, very good position to be in.

**How?** There are two easy parts to this strategy: (1) just talk, and (2) try to contribute great questions/comments.

The first should be pretty easy. You can ask questions or make comments as they come to you naturally during a lecture. However, you'll get super mega bonus points if you talk during awkward silences. You know the kind I'm talking about: the professor asks a question, and everyone just sits there looking at t their notebooks. *That's the best time to talk.* If you're the one who tackles those silences, and you do it in a productive way, your professors will love you, and if they love you, you'll get much better grades.

So how do you ask a good question? How to contribute a good comment? The easiest way is to try to contribute things that *move the conversation forward*. That could mean any number of things. Before you offer your question or comment, ask yourself the following:

- Will this help everyone in the class understand better?
- Is this something important that hasn't been said yet?
- Is it fun or interesting?

If the answers to any of these is *yes*, you're probably good, so fire away!

**Pro tip!** Don't contribute bad questions/comments! Those are usually the ones that don't add anything, make the teacher go on tangents or the like. This is how you get those negative brownie points. No thanks.

# Writing Hacks

This is my primary area of expertise, having been a college writing instructor for so many years. Most people absolutely *hate* writing, which, to me, is a shame because I love it so much. This chapter is about how to write great papers very easily and very fast.

# Hack #15: **Not BS'ing** is easier and will get you better grades.

Listen, we've all done it. We're writing that paper, and it feels like we've absolutely run out of things to say. So we go back through, racking our brain for more *stuff* to say. A few extra words here. A few extra sentences there. Finally, we stop right at the prescribed word count and turn it in.

Having taught lots of college classes myself, I can tell you that most professors have a finely tuned BS detector. Personally, as soon as I detected some BS, the grade dropped immediately because it told me that the student stopped trying.

However, when I was a student, I had that same problem: running out of stuff to say. So I found a pretty good way to get around without BS'ing that is actually **easier** than making stuff up.

**IN A NUTSHELL: If you run out of stuff to say, simply find a new fact and pop it into the appropriate part of the paper.**

**Why?** The goal of any paper is to demonstrate what you know and what you think about a subject. If you start BS'ing, it demonstrates exactly the opposite: that you don't know enough to squeeze out 50 extra words worth of useful information. Even worse, it shows that you don't even have any more thoughts of your own on the matter.

Additionally, BS'ing your way through a paper usually doesn't save you time. It often doesn't even save you effort, which makes it even worse than lazy—it makes it crazy.

The good news is that *not BS'ing is really, really easy.* Not only is it easy, but it will set you apart from the half of your class who thinks they can get away with it. It's win-win situation. It's easier, and it will get you a better grade.

**How?** The best way to avoid BS if you feel like you've run out of stuff to say is to just go find a new fact. Just one. From anywhere. Scan your paper and see where that fact fits in. Then, plop it in. After you plop it in, add some sort of commentary—a few sentences on why you added it, why it's important, and how it pertains to the rest of the essay.

Adding *just one fact* in this way takes 10 minutes and gives you an extra 200 words. Still need more stuff to say? Add another fact! Or just expand your discussion of the first fact.

The idea here is that if you don't have much to say, you are much, much better off adding *new* information instead of just repeating something you've already said. Plus, it's easier to just plop a good fact in than it is to make something up.

**Shortcut:** Often, you don't even have to add a new fact. You can just go to any section of your paper and—instead of adding a new fact—ask a new question and speculate about the answer. This is slightly more difficult but requires no research. For example, if your paper is about dog training, and you've already written about the best methods, take a second to think-aloud-on-paper about why the best ones are the best. Adding your own, thoughtful commentary *still counts as adding new information.*

## Hack #16: **Overshoot the length** of your papers, even if it's just a little.

When I was teaching college classes, I spent a lot of time grading papers, so I developed a lot of little hacks for that, too. One of the best ones was this: when I picked up a paper to grade it, I'd flip to the back to see if the paper was long or short. If it was short, that paper was almost always worse than the long ones.

Why was this the case? Well, if you don't care enough to even hit the word count, you probably didn't care enough to write a thoughtful paper. Likewise, students who wrote longer papers—even if they weren't the best papers—were usually trying harder.

Obviously, this wasn't the only thing I looked at, but it was a very strong signal about the student's attitude towards the paper, and I could use it as my first litmus test before I even started reading.

**IN A NUTSHELL: Always overshoot the length of your papers, even if it's just by a little, because it shows you're trying harder, which is a strong quality signal to most teachers.**

**Why?** The reality is that some students try harder than others, and about 80% of the time, the students who are trying harder do much better work. So, many teachers and professors will find ways to quickly check to see how hard a student tried.

If you can give a teacher some of these signals, you can essentially say to them "Hey, I took this seriously." And that counts for a lot. Grading, whether we like it or not, is largely subjective, especially when it comes to stuff like papers. And that makes all of those little quality signals more important.

It also makes something as easy as going just a tiny bit long on your paper both very easy and very powerful.

**How?** Just go long. This one isn't rocket surgery. Take 10 extra minutes and write a few extra paragraphs. You don't have to write a novel. In fact, that's probably counter-productive. You just have to go a tiny bit over.

Most of the time, this just means expanding the trains of thought you've already developed in a paper. Remember, you can add extra words *anywhere* in a paper; it doesn't just have to be at the end.

However, you can also use our anti-BS technique from the previous tip. That works really well here.

**Important note!** Don't go *too* long. If your paper is several pages longer than it has to be, you're just making extra work for your teacher, who will certainly not appreciate it. So, even though going a tiny bit long can make you look like a more serious student, going even longer does not make you look better.

In fact, it can have the opposite effect: it can make you look like you don't follow directions, which turns your quality signal into a big flashing sign that says, "I know better than you."

# Hack #17: Cut your paper writing time in half.

This is my domain. I have several degrees in writing, and I taught college writing classes for some time, so I know paper writing inside and out.

So believe me when I say that most people hate writing papers. It's true. I've run across very few people who yell, "Yes!" when they're assigned a paper. Why? Because it almost always takes a really long time.

Luckily, I've developed something of a system over the years, and you can use it to drastically reduce the time you spend on writing. It takes a bit of willpower, but if you do it, you can literally cut paper writing time in half.

**IN A NUTSHELL: Cut your paper writing time in half by batching your research, writing a simple outline, and word-purging.**

**Why?** There are really three tactics here. The first is *batching* your research. Basically, that means is doing all of your research at once. It's a bit more than that, though. It really means doing the research *and then organizing all of the materials you'll need for the paper and put them right in front of you.*

That's the most important thing. If you just gather and organize your materials, you should be able to do all of your research for any paper (outside of a master's thesis or a doctoral dissertation) in about 10 minutes.

Secondly, you want to write a good outline. And I'm not talking about just any outline. I'm talking about the simplest possible outline. Your outline should take no more than a few minutes, and it should never be longer than a page. In fact, if you outline the way I describe below, your outlines will usually be about 10 lines long. That's it

Finally, all of that stuff you just did—getting your research materials ready and writing the simplest possible outline—is all meant to help you word-purge, which basically means writing without thinking. I'll tell you how to do that here in a second, but the idea is to basically treat your papers like a freewriting exercise.

**How should you research?** Remember, our goal here is to organize everything we need in about 10 minutes. In general, you should know the books you need to research and at least have a vague idea of the most important sections.

When you set out to organize your research, first, organize it from most important source to least important source. When you have 3-4 good sources, *stop.* You should almost never use more than that (unless your professor asks you to, of course). It just gets jumbled.

Now that you've got 3-4 source materials organized from most important (or useful) to least important go through and take a quick look at the most relevant information in those sources and bookmark it. Ideally, you will have made some notes already, which will make this part even faster.

You'll want to mark 3-4 things in each source and probably no more. Remember, a good paper doesn't just have tons of source material, it *builds* on it.

**How should you outline?** Outlining is something almost everyone gets wrong. Why? Because they put in *way* too many details!

A good outline should almost never be more than 10 lines long. Here are a few rules.

Write your main argument at the top. Then, write a bullet for each part of that argument; let's call these *sections*. Under each section, write one bullet that captures the main point of each paragraph in that section.

The best way to think of an outline is that the sections should be the *shortest possible version of the argument*. When you write the sections, it should feel like your grandma just asked you what your paper was about, and you have to tell her about it in 30 seconds before she gets bored. The most important thing here is to keep it super simple.

Here's an example of what that might look like:

- **Argument:** French revolutionaries were heavily influenced by coffee.
- **Section 1:** Before coffee, the French mostly drank wine.
  - Why the French drank wine
  - How much wine they drank
  - Effect on the culture
- **Section 2:** Coffee introduced a new kind of culture.
  - Coffee houses sprang up
  - People were energized instead of drunk
  - It was exotic, new and exciting
- **Section 3:** This new culture was much more concerned with politics and much more active.
  - Because people were energized instead of drunk, they were thinking about stuff more
  - Coffee houses were inherently social
  - Coffee houses were also intellectual and attracted smart people
- **Section 4:** This was a factor in people getting angrier taking part in revolutionary activities.
  - Major political minds met in coffee houses
  - People talked to other people and gathered support for various movements
  - Some of those movements turned into a full-blown revolution
- **Section 5:** Coffee is awesome and has more historical significance than I thought!
  - Pretty crazy that coffee had that kind of impact
  - Makes me appreciate coffee in a whole new light

That outline took me about 5 minutes, and, since you'd be adding evidence and examples from your source materials for each of those bullets, it could easily yield a 5-7 page paper. In reality, it would be very easy to get a 10-page paper out of this.

So far, we've organized all our research materials and written an outline, and it's taken no more than 15 minutes.

**How should you word-purge (write)?** This is the thing that is going to be hardest for most people, but hopefully, the research materials and the outline should help a lot.

The idea of word-purging is to write without stopping. That can be really difficult, but if you can do it, you can finish 90% of a paper really, really quickly.

Here's the secret: *whenever you feel stuck, steal and rewrite things from your sources and your outline.*

As you're writing, you're going to feel stuck sometimes. When that happens, immediately reach for either your outline or your sources. Then, find something interesting that fits with what you're writing and plop it in.

If it's a quote, put that in. If it's an idea, put that in. Here's the important part: after you put it in, *riff on it*. Ask yourself, "What do I think about this, and why is it important?" Then, just answer those questions in written form under the paragraphs.

Here's the best part: as long as you're citing your sources, it's not even cheating! In fact, that's exactly what most of your professors want you to do!

So, if you're stuck, plop something in from a source and riff on it. Just don't stop writing. If you use this method, you should be able to knock most papers out in an hour or less (depending on how fast you type).

**How should you revise?** There's one revision tactic that is super easy and works almost all of the time. If you use it, you should never have to revise another way again. Fair warning, though: it's going to make you feel kind of silly. Ready?

Read your whole paper aloud.

I've given that advice to all of my students and all of my employees, and hardly anyone every takes it. But trust me when I say it's the single best thing you can do for you papers.

By reading a paper aloud, you'll catch *so* many more mistakes than you would have otherwise. Even more importantly, though, you'll catch inconsistencies in your logic.

Finally, it's just super-efficient. Normally, if you read your whole paper aloud, you only have to revise one time, and you're done.

When you do read aloud, you want to pay attention to any parts that make you go, "Wait… what?" Those are the parts that need work. Then, just fix them!

This is the method I've used to write all my papers in both graduate school and undergraduate school. I've also used this method to write nearly all of my professional pieces, which is well over 1,000 articles.

It works!

# Biology Hacks

Finally, here are some biology hacks. A lot of people forget that your brain is part of your body, which is a pretty complex system that has to be maintained if you want it to operate at its optimal performance level. This chapter is about taking care of the machine in order to make everything else we've discussed happen more smoothly.

## Hack #18: **Don't cram all night**. It's bad for your neurons. Do this instead…

All-night cram sessions are as much of the lore of college as kegs, fraternities and protests. And, believe me, I'm as guilty of cramming all my studying into one night as anyone else—mostly because, when I first started college, I was still a *huge* procrastinator.

However, I quickly learned that it was a terrible strategy if I actually wanted to do well GPA-wise. I didn't know why, though. But now I do! So check it out.

**IN A NUTSHELL: As much as possible, try to never cram all night before a test. Instead, even if you procrastinated, try to study in small sessions throughout the day and early that morning.**

**Why?** I think a lot of people have intuitively known that cramming all night before an exam is a bad strategy, but now there's some science to back it up.

In the May issue of the *Journal of Neuroscience*, scientists from Carnegie Mellon (a team led by Alison L. Barth if you want to look it up) showed that if you repeatedly subject your brain to the same stimuli over and over again, you can actually *shrink* the synapses.

That's basically a fancy way of saying you're going to remember what you're trying to learn for a much shorter time than if you hadn't done that. If you're particularly unlucky, you may even forget it *before* the test. If that happens, you've just stayed up all night for nothing!

Plus, being well-rested before an exam is just plain old common sense, right? Regardless of what you're doing, if it's important, it's probably better to be well-rested.

**How?** This is going to take a bit of planning on your part, but it's not that difficult, and it certainly doesn't have to be stressful. Here's what worked for me.

If I knew I had a big test coming up, I'd just carry my notes around with me a day or two before. Whenever I had a spare moment, I'd do a bit of studying. Nothing intense. Just some simple techniques that you'll find in this book (e.g. mnemonic devices, saying things out loud).

Most importantly, though, I'd only do this for 5 minutes or so at a time. That way, I was creating a *strong* connection to the ideas I was trying to remember instead of basically battering them into my brain.

Then, instead of staying up all night before the test, I'd *go to bed early and wake up early in the morning*. I'd spend the morning doing a more intense study session. This helps make everything fresh (not to mention riding on a glorious caffeinated wave of coffee).

By the time I'd gone to take the test, I'd created some strong mental connections by studying lightly throughout the day before, and I'd just gone over all the material a few times that morning after getting lots of rest, eating a great breakfast and drinking some coffee.

This is a much, much better strategy than cramming all night. Plus, it's about a million times less stressful. Also, it usually ends up taking a lot less time.

**Pro tip:** If you're a super procrastinator and you don't even have any notes yet, try to start two days before hand and carry your book around instead. When you take your short, 5-minute study breaks, use the first day to make notes from the book, and then use the second day going over them. Easy!

# Hack #19: **Exercise while studying** to boost your memory.

This is one of t hose awesome little bio-hacks that has lots of benefits outside of studying. Everyone knows exercise is awesome, but not many know that it can boost your learning power by quite a bit.

**IN A NUTSHELL: Doing some light during studying can help you remember whatever it is your reading, especially if you're trying to remember it a week or two later.**

**Why?** This section may be a tad disappointing. We have a ton of studies that show this works, but we have very little that show *why* it works. And that's not surprising. The brain has always been super hard to understand, and this phenomenon is no exception.

It's still cool, though. One of the most important studies was published in *PLoS One* in May 2013. The study observed 81 healthy women at different levels of activity during study. So, one group (the control) studied a new set of vocabulary without exercising at all. The second studied while performing some light exercise. And the third studied while performing exercise at a higher intensity (not vigorous, but higher).

Two days later, the women were tested on the vocabulary they studied. And everyone did okay (they all remembered *some* of the information). However, the second group, who exercised lightly, remembered significantly more words than the other group.

A second study by the American College of Sports Medicine in Indianapolis found that, while exercising does help memory retention, it *does not help* immediately after the exercise. It's most effective when the person is at least a day later.

In fact, in this study, the people who exercised actually performed *worse*. Obviously, you don't want that, so it pays to realize that timing is important here.

**How?** So what's the takeaway here? Basically, if it's at all possible, try exercising while you study. And don't make it some weird, crazy, obstacle-course workout or something. It should be light. In the above studies, the participants were lightly riding a bike.

Try to do this consistently. If you're a workout nut anyway, it shouldn't be a problem at all. Just take your study stuff with you when you work out.

If you're not a person who likes to workout, just taking your study materials on a simple walk around your neighborhood will have the same effect.

The major upside of this, of course, is that you're totally killing two birds with one stone here. You're getting your workout in and studying at the same time! That's a lot of time saved. Plus, you'll probably get that awesome feeling of accomplishment that comes after either studying or working out—only it'll be doubled!

**Pro tip!** Don't work out the day you are going to take an exam.  Remember, that second study found that people actually performed worse when quizzed right after studying, but their memory was better a few days later when their body was at rest.

So, exercise when you study, but don't do squat on the day of the test!

## Conclusion

Studying better is almost always about studying smarter, not harder. In fact, if you study efficiently, you'll end up spending a lot less time with your nose in the books, which will end up making you feel a lot better about life in general, and you'll likely see a major boost in your grades.

If you enjoyed this book, please stop by and see us over at Learnu.org, where we write about college degrees, careers and salaries in addition to awesome resources like this book.

See you there!